Florence Nightingale

by

John N. Merrill

Maps, photographs and pencil sketches by John N. Merrill

"I hike the footpaths and trails of the world for others to enjoy."

2010

My Derbyshire History Series
~ Famous Derbyshire People

THE JOHN MERRILL FOUNDATION

THE JOHN MERRILL FOUNDATION
32, Holmesdale, Waltham Cross, Hertfordshire, England. EN8 8QY

Tel/Fax - 01992-762776
E-mail - marathonhiker@aol.com
www. johnmerrillwalkguides.com

A catalogue record for this book is available from the British Library.

Typset and designed by *The John Merrill Foundation*
Printed and handmade by *John N. Merrill.*

©Text and routes - John N. Merrill, HonMUniv, 2007.
© Maps, Photographs & pencil sketches - John N. Merrill, HonMUniv, 2007.

ISBN 978 -1-903627-18-4
First published - November 2001. Reprinted & revised - July 2007.
Special limited edition.

Typeset in Humanst521 - bold, italic, and plain 11pt, 14pt and 18pt
Main titles in 18pt .**Humanst521 Bd BT** by John Merrill in
Adobe Pagemaker on a Apple Macintosh.

Please note - *The maps in this guide are purely illustrative. You are encouraged to use the appropriate 1:25,000 O.S. Explorer map as detailed on each walk.*

John Merrill has walked all the routes in this book and detailed what he found. Meticulous research has been undertaken to ensure that this publication is highly accurate at the time of going to press. The publishers, however, cannot be held responsible for alterations, errors, omissions, or for changes in details given. They would welcome information to help keep the book up to date.

Cover photograph - Early sketch of Florence Nightingale (front) and Lea Hurst - by John Merrill.

2

Over the last 40 years John Merrill has walked over 200,000 miles - more than ten times around the world , wearing out 108 pairs of boots in the process. He has completed a remarkable and unequalled number of marathon walks - walking more than 28 miles per day on average - including being the first person to walk around Britain - 7,000 miles - in ten months. He has walked across Europe, Africa, India, Nepal, Asia, America, and along the great trails of America and Canada. He has completed many Pilgrim routes to Santiago de Compostela, Canterbury, Walsingham and Trondheim in Norway. Many more marathons and pilgrimages are planned.

He has written more than 320 guidebooks to his walks, most of which he prints and publishes himself. After his coast walk he realised the fame game prevented his from doing what he was destined to do, and that was to simply walk and write. He purposefully left the stage and concentrated on what he wanted to do. He does not consult anyone, promote or seek publicity; preferring to follow his own quiet spiritual path through life. This means he can write a book, on average one every month. He is not beholden to anyone, just a free spirit, with no staff, agents or editors. As a result he is not rich in money terms but in life and places walked to, a millionaire.

He is not a loner, quite the reverse, but to get the material and accomplish his walks - *"he who travels alone, travels fastest"*. And, by going alone you never forget. He is guided and has a very deep spiritual faith and has never come to any harm or put a foot wrong. The only way to be close to nature and mother earth and see its huge variety, is by walking; no other sport/ exercise gives you that connectedness to the earth. He does no research beforehand, preferring to walk around the corner and come to a church, historic house, sacred site etc., and discover for himself their secrets. To be aware of what's next is to dampen the impact.

> *"A journey of a thousand miles, begins with a single step."*
> Lao Tzu (The Tao Te Ching).

I am on my third stage of my journey as an intuitive master, which continues daily - one life is not enough.

> *"Do not seek fame. Do not make plans.*
> *Do not be absorbed by activities.*
> *Do not think that you know.*
> *Be aware of all that is and dwell in the infinite.*
> *Wander where there is no path.*
> *Be all that heaven gave you, but act as though*
> *you have received nothing.*
> *Be empty, that is all."*   Chuang Tzu

3

CONTENTS

INTRODUCTION

The Florence Nightingale story is a classic tale of how a person's commitment and desire leads to the very summit of achievement; it is a path that few tread. Unlike many rags to riches stories, she already came from a substantial background, but it was the forces of acceptance that where to prove her greatest battles. Women from her background were meant to marry and be host to her husband ambitions, but this was not for her. She knew in her teens her calling and strove to attain them. Her parents were against her ideas and desires, especially her mother who sought a husband for her and sent her abroad to forget her ideas. None of which worked as Florence continued to stick rigidly to her calling and continued to lay foundations.

When the time came she rose to the challenge and demonstrated that women were upto the task and could achieve so much with so little. Within three years she became a legend and England was proud of her. Even her parents agreed she had been right to forge her own path and basked in her glory. But in keeping with so many exceptional people, she wanted no fuss and upon her return to England from Crimea, she came incognito as Miss Smith, and stole quietly to Lea Hurst to continue the next stage of her work. Although she had almost burnt herself out helping the wounded and sick, being *"The Lady with the Lamp"*, many thought she would not live long. But again she dumbfounded everyone and worked harder than ever and lived another fifty years, outliving them all.

Hers is a fascinating and compelling story whose legacy remains today. Absorb and learn from her achievements and then explore Nightingale country and follow paths that she and her family once trod.

Happy reading and exploring!
John N. Merrill

Florence Nightingale

"A Lady with a lamp shall stand.
In the great history of the land;
A noble type of good
Heroic womanhood."

Longfellow.

Early Life -

Florence was born in Villa Colombia, Florence, Italy on May 12th. 1820, the second daughter of Fanny and William Edward Shore. Like her sister, Parthenope, who was born in Naples in 1819, she was given the Christian name of her place of birth. In Parthenope case it is the Greek name of birthplace, Naples. The surname, Nightingale, was soon changed from Shore, following William's inheritance of Lea Hurst Estate from his Uncle, Peter Nightingale, when only 21. His uncle was known locally as *"Mad Peter"*, because of his reckless horsemanship.

William Edward Shore (Nightingale) studied at Cambridge and was described as a *"clever but lazy student."* Fanny was over thirty years old when she married William in 1817. Her father, William Smith, would eventually spend 46 years in the House of Commons and was an ardent fighter for the plight of the factory workers who were overworked and underpaid.

The house that William inherited was small and in poor condition. Following the family's return from Florence, he began designing the present building. The porch bears the date 1825 and it is believed that they had already moved in by then. While the work was going on they lived on the eastern side of Lea, in another of their properties, Lea Hall. Fanny had already decided that Lea Hurst was not big enough for them and cold in winter. In 1825 William purchased Embley Park in Hampshire. The family now divided their time between the two estates, with summer at Lea

6

Embley Park.

Hurst and winter in Hampshire. Embley was chosen as it was near Fanny's two married sisters, Mrs Nicholson at Farnham and Mrs Bonham Carter at Winchester. Embley was more of a social home while at Lea Hurst, William indulged in hunting, shooting and fishing. He was also very attentive to his tenants, providing a school.

Florence's schooling was by an able Governess who taught her Greek, Latin, French and Italian together with history and mathematics. She was also adept at music and drawing. Her mother taught her that it was their duty to help the poor. Florence enjoyed visiting the sick and helping out and when young used to dress her dolls up as patients. Later people she visited would recall that she was, *"Better than any doctor."* The seeds were sown and from an early age knew she had to accomplish something good for the world; marriage would not be fulfilling. Her father was her confidant and agreed that women should equally share the work.

On February 7th. 1837 when aged 17, Florence, who was deeply religious and prayed everyday, suddenly knew that God was calling her to become a nurse.It would be another thirteen years before

7

her ambitions began to be realised. Hospitals were quite primitive at this time and were not the place for a woman, especially one from her privileged background. Her mother was aghast at her ideas and told her it was her duty to marry and serve her husband not the sick. A suitable man was looked for and to take her mind off her dreams the family went abroad in September 1837 for two years, to France, Italy and Switzerland, in an attempt to eradicate them. But, she remained steadfast in her goal.

Florence grew up in a privileged background but despite the social whirl, she remained a quiet, shy and lonely child preferring her own company. She enjoyed music and opera and while on holiday in Italy in 1838, she went to the opera two or three times a week. Many believe that this period of her life from 1838 to 1842 were her happiest. She also formed a friendship with Richard Monkcton Milnes (later Lord Houghton), heir to a large estate in Yorkshire. But, despite her mother's attempts, over three years, to see them married, they never did.

Back at Lea Hurst in 1843, Florence spent as much time as she could helping the poor and sick, often getting food and clothes from her mother. When it was time to move south to Embley, Florence did not want to go, *"It breaks my heart to leave Lea Hurst"*, she wrote.

Early Nursing Days -

Her goal was now defined and when any members of the family became ill she took control and nursed them back to health. Although not able to get proper training because of her mother's disapproval, she spent her time actively involved in reading and learning as much as she could. Her mother said such work was for the "lower orders" and not suitable work for a lady. Florence asked her parents to allow her to go to work at Salisbury Hospital under the physician, Dr. Fowler, but she met with strong opposition.

In 1842 she met de Bunsen, the Prussian Ambassador in London, who told her about the work of Pastor Theodore Fliedner at Kaiserwerth near Dusseldorf (Germany). Four years later the Kaiserwerth Institute was recognised by the state. The rules were severe - you had to serve for five years without pay; could only be accepted if unmarried and under the age of 25; and expected to devote oneself to nursing. Her parents were opposed to her going and rather than cause a rift in the family bided her time.

While at Embley Park in 1844, she met Dr. Howe and his wife, Julia Ward Howe. She told them of her desire to become a nurse and Dr. Howe replied, "*My dear Miss Florence it would be unusual and in England whatever is unusual is thought to be unsuitable; but I say to you, go forward if you have a vocation for that way of life. Act up to that inspiration, and you will find that there is never anything unbecoming nor unladylike in doing your duty for the good of others.*"

Florence was aware that the Roman Catholic Church had teachings on nursing but she was a devotee of the Church of England and could not accept the Catholic tradition. In 1847 she went abroad to Italy with the Bracebridge family in an attempt by her parents to rid her of her "*mad notions*". It was not to succeed. Instead the trip proved very fortuitous for in Rome she met Dr. Manning, Mary Stanley and Sidney Herbert. The later was to prove a major person in her life.

Pastor Fliedner.

Upon returning to England in the summer of 1848 she was more determined than ever. In the Autumn with her parents approval she visited London hospitals and help assist in the organisation of ragged schools. A year later she went abroad again with the Bracebridge's to Italy, Egypt and Greece, but only agreed to the trip provided that she would be allowed to visit the Kaiserwerth Institute on their way back. She finally reached the Institute in July 1850 and was most impressed. She decided she wanted to be trained here under Pastor Fliender guidance and then establish a similar Institute in England. She wrote a pamphlet, anonymously titled, *"The Institute of Kaiserwerth on the Rhine"*, published in 1851.

1851 was the year of the Great Exhibition in the Crystal Palace, designed by Joseph Paxton - another "Famous Derbyshire Person." Florence did not enjoy the social scene there and was glad to leave with her mother to Germany, where she would go to Kaiserwerth for three months. Here she met Sidney Herbert who fully approved of her decision. She turned out to be a good student but found the nursing limited, but convinced even more of her goals.

Sidney Herbert - later Lord Herbert of Lea.

Back in England the family battles for her vocation continued. With the help of Sidney Herbert she went to Paris in February 1853 to the Maison de la Providence under the care of the Sisters of Charity. She was not here long before being called back to England to nurse her Grandmother. Following her death in May she returned to Paris and caught measles! Returning to England she made a firm stand with parents, telling them they would no longer interfere with her career.

A vacancy for a Superintendent of *"The Establishment for Gentlewomen during illness"* was advertised. Florence accepted the post with Sidney Herbert's support. Her father agreed to support her and gave her an allowance of £500 per annum and she took rooms in Pall Mall. In August 1853 she began work at 1, Upper Harley Street. She soon proved her amazing and natural skills and was soon asking for a larger place to train nurses. She reorganised the hospital but found the committee work hindered change. She was loved by her patients and the doctors too realised her talents were wasted here. Florence knew that nurses needed to be trained and how hospitals should be run. She reorganised the nursing at King's College Hospital. When cholera broke out in 1854, Florence volunteered as Superintendent of Nurses at Middlesex Hospital. Here she worked day and night and it became clear to everyone that this was her calling. But before anything more could be done, the Crimean War had started.

The Crimean War -

Hostilities began in 1853 between Russia and Turkey, with Britain backing the Turks. When the Russians destroyed the Turkish fleet at Sinope on November 3rd. 1853, strong feelings in Britain and France were aroused leading to a declaration of war on Russia on March 28th 1854. The battle was centred around the Crimean Peninsula in particular the Russian fortress at Sebastopol. In September British troops landed on the peninsula but were soon routed by in a series of famous battles at Alma, Balaclava and Inkerman - the fiercest and hardest battle of the war. The battle of Balaclava - (October 25th 1854) is recorded in Lord Alfred Tennyson's poem - *The Charge of the Light Brigade.* Here the British Light Cavalrymen charged against Russian artillery, with very heavy losses - 600 died. Whilst the death and injuries were very substantial more died from cholera.

Originally it was thought to be a short campaign but the advantage gained in the Battle of Alma was not pursued and the war dragged on for nearly three years. The Russians were able to prepare to withstand a long siege of Sebastopol.

Sidney Herbert the Secretary of State for War, asked Florence for help. She readily agreed - her moment had come - and the Cabinet approved her appointment to work with the Army Hospital Commission. News of her appointment caused a sensation for never before had a woman been so honoured. Her parents, although belatedly, were justly proud of their daughter. Florence gathered a team of forty nurses, including Mrs. Bracebridge, together and set off on October 21st. 1854, to Scutari where the hospital was.

She arrived in November 4th. 1854 to find there were little supplies or furniture in the General Hospital and Barrack Hospital. Between them they could accommodate 1,000 patients, which was believed to be large enough; it wasn't. The doctor's disliked seeing women in their world. But all this would change dramatically. The injured and dying were brought by boat across the Black Sea to the hospital; a journey of seven to ten days, resulting in more deaths en route. Generally there was one doctor on board and on average 74 out of 1,000 died on the crossing. With such a flood of patients

The cemetry and hospital at Scutari.

the doctors were grateful for all the help they could get. What happened next has become a legend. Florence reorganised the hospital which grew to the size of a small town with thousands of sick and injured men. She worked often twenty-four hours a day and became the *"Lady with lamp."* Her nurses were affectionally called *"Nightingales".*

Queen Victoria took great interest in the war effort and especially the work of Florence and her Nightingales. In a letter dated 6th. December 1854 to Sidney Herbert she wrote -

"Let Mrs. Herbert also know that I wish Miss Nightingale and the ladies would tell these poor, noble wounded and sick men that no one takes a warmer interest or feels more for their sufferings or admires their courage and heroism more than their Queen. Day and night she thinks of her beloved troops. So does the Prince." Victoria.

Florence worked relentlessly looking after and supervising the nursing of the wounded and sick. She visited the wards carrying her lantern. Often she would sit on the bed of patient while they dictated a letter home. She wrote countless letters for others and

14

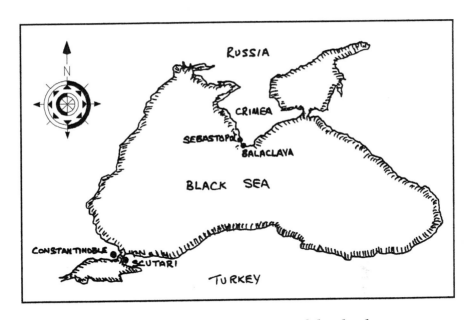

wrote letters of sympathy to the parents of the dead.

Florence soon became named, *"The Lady in Chief"*, as she began to reorganise the hospital - Barrack Hospital had 2,000 patients. She saw that the key to reducing the deaths were a vast improvement in the sanitation and ventilation. The food was poor; supplies inadequate and mismanaged. She continually wrote to Sidney Herbert asking for supplies, giving detailed reports and how her reorganisations were going. He did his utmost to improve matters. Land for a cemetery was arranged and a commission to look into the sanitary conditions began work in February 1856. There findings agreed with Florence's proposals and her work had, *"saved the British Army."* She had demonstrated that by good nursing and improved sanitation improved people's recovery rate.

Reports of the food conditions appeared in The Times, leading to the notable chef of the Reform Club, Alexis Soyer, to come over at his own expense to sort the kitchens out, in April 1855. He soon carried out many beneficial reforms. He admired Florence and wrote - *"With matters of the most grave import, a gentle smile passes radiantly over her countenance, thus proving her evenness of temper; at other times, when wit or a pleasantry prevails, the heroine is lost in the happy, good-natured smile which pervades*

15

Florence writing a letter for a soldier.

her face, and you recognise only the charming woman."

When Florence first arrived at Scutari 42% of the patients died from their wounds from disease due to the poor sanitation. Six months later she had reduced this figure down to little over 2%. In May 1855 , with the numbers arriving from the battle front considerably less, she decided to go to the Balaclava Hospital in the Crimea. Her work was already showing considerable results and stories drifted back to the front about her. Upon arriving at the Crimea a large group were waiting to welcome and see her. She was accompanied by Mrs. Bracebridge and Alexis Soyer. Together they inspected the hospitals around Sebastopol and made many recommendations to their improvement. So far she had escaped contacting Crimean Fever, but after being in such close contact to others suffering from it, she finally succumbed to the fever. News spread of her illness and many thought she would die. Even obituaries appeared in the London papers. A troop of weeping soldiers carried her back to Scutari. After two weeks she began to recover and convalesced on a yatch, The New London.

Early 1855 the government changed and Sidney Herbert was no longer at the War office, but insisted that Florence should still write her reports to him and he would do what he could.

Sebastopol finally fell on the 8th. September 1855 but instead of returning to England she elected to stay here and carry on her work. 20,000 English soldiers had died during the war but only 5,000 on the battlefield. Queen Victoria remarked, *"Such a clear head, I wish we had her at the War Office."* In November 1855 plans were made to create a fund - The Nightingale Hospital Fund. The fund raised £44,000. Florence was now a legend and back in England her portrait was bought in large numbers; decorated shop windows; new babies were christened Florence; songs were written and racehorses named.

In January 1856 Queen Victoria wrote to her from Windsor Castle-

"You are, I know, well aware of the high sense I entertain of the Christian devotion which you have displayed during this great and bloody war, and I need hardly repeat to you how warm my admiration is for your services, which are fully equal to those of my dear and brave soldiers, whose sufferings you have had the privilege of alleviating in so merciful a manner."

With the letter was a diamond brooch designed by Prince Albert. On the front were the words - *"Crimea"* and *"Blessed are the merciful."* She is reportedly to have worn the brooch only once.

She stayed until the end of the war when a Peace Treaty was signed in Paris on March 30th 1856. She had by this time made life much more comfortable for her patients, with a cafe, reading and writing rooms, classes and lectures arranged. There little left for her to do. It was time to return to England, but was aware of the reception plans. The Sultan of Egypt presented her with a diamond bracelet and money to divided between the nurses and hospitals. The British Government put a Man-o'-War for her use. But she did not want this attention; what she had done was her duty. She set off back incognito as Miss Smith, and weary from her efforts slipped quietly back to Derbyshire to continue he life's work, on August 5th. 1856. Even her parents did not know of her arrival.

It is interesting to note that the hat factory at Lea Bridge made military hats for the soldiers in the Crimean War. Also, Sir Joseph Whitworth, later of Darley Dale, made 0.45 calibre rifles and ammunition for the soldiers.

After Crimea -

Once settled back in England, she spent most of her time in London, devoting herself to the improvement of nursing. Her time in Crimea had seriously depleted her strength and she was now semi-invalid, making her believe she had not long to live. Florence infact lived another fifty years and accomplished a great deal. She preferred to work and had little time for honours or celebrations for the work she had done. Having proved that by good nursing and sanitation how patients soon regained their health, she wanted to continue this work.

In the autumn of 1856 she visited Queen Victoria at Balmoral and during there meeting urged that the medical service in the army be investigated. Six months later a commission was set up with Sidney Herbert appointed as the commissioner. Florence served as a member of the commission. Many of the proposals were based on hers.

Her sister, Parthenope (Parthe), aged 40 married in June 1858, becoming Lady Verney. Her husband was a wealthy widower with four children.

Florence spent her time writing on hospital organisation, training schools for nurses and midwives, helping to establish today's nursing profession. In 1858 was published her major work - *"Notes on Matters Affecting the Health, Efficiency, and Hospital Administration of the British Army."* The following year, in 1859, her book, *"Notes on Nursing"* was published. In the space of a month, 15,000 were sold.

In 1859 Sidney Herbert was back at the War Office and immediately began reorganising everything along the principals and discussions with Florence. These included sanitation, ventilation and preventative medicine. The annual mortalitity rate among soldiers at home was still high - 175 in 1,000. The work load and the constant urging of improvement by Florence, led to his exhaustion and he resigned in December 1860. For his service he was made Lord Herbert of Lea, but died in 1861. His final words were - *"Poor Florence! Poor Florence! Our joint work unfinished."*

Florence in her middle years.

In 1860 she established a school for training nurses, laying the foundations of modern nursing training. The Nightingale Fund was used and in June 24 pupils started a year's training at St. Thomas's hospital, London - the site is now the Florence Nightingale Museum - 2, Lambeth Palace Road, London. SE1 7EW. The training was a great success and other centres opened both here and abroad.

Florence turned her attention to India and its high death rate. In 1863 she wrote a paper - *"How people may live and not die in India."* Ten years later, following the sanitary reform she wrote another paper - *"How some people have lived and not died in India."*

Henri Dunant, had seen how effective Florence's work had been in the Crimea and in 1864 the Geneva Convention was drawn up and the Red Cross established.

By the year 1872 Florence felt she had completed her life's work of reforming nursing, but still carried on working as hard as ever. Her father died in January 1874, aged 84, leaving her depressed. She returned to Lea Hurst to look after her mother.

Ten years later on April 23rd. 1883, Queen Victoria instituted the Royal Red Cross and Florence was selected as the first recipient of the award. Four years later District Nursing was started and spread throughout the country. On May 12th. 1890 her sister, Parthe died. In 1900 on her 80th birthday, congratulations from all the world, reached her. She continued to work hard but eventually agreed she should have secretary to help with her letters. A nurse also came to look after her and a story is told that after she had been tucked into bed, she would get out and tuck the nurse in!

In November 1907, aged 87, she was presented at her bedside, the Order of Merit by King Edward V1 1, the first woman to receive the award. Earlier in the year she had been honoured by the International Conference of Red Cross Societies. The following year in 1908 she was given the Freedom of the City of London, a rare honour for a woman.

On August 13th. 1910, aged 90, she peacefully passed away. Everyone wanted her to buried in Westminster Abbey, but her wishes were observed and she was buried in the family grave at East Wellow. She had left instructions that her funeral, like her life, be simple and no fuss, with just two people attending. But, being the legend and heroine she was people from around the world came to pay their final homage to one of the most remarkable women of England. Her simple headstone reads -

"F.N. born 1820
Died 1910."

I am myself always a prisoner from illness & overwork . but all the more Livies for godspeed

Florence Nightingale

Sample of Florence's handwriting and signature.

Historical plaque in Holloway.

A walk around Lea, Holloway and Dethick - 5 miles.

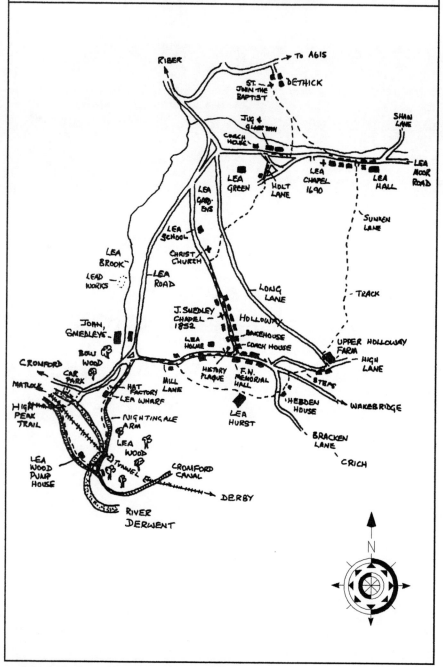

24

A WALK AROUND LEA, HOLLOWAY AND DETHICK
- 5 MILES
- allow 3 or more hours.

Route - High Peak Junction Car Park - Cromford Canal - Nightingale Arm - Canal Wharf - Mill Lane - Lea Hurst - Holloway - Upper Holloway - Lea Hall - Lea Chapel - Dethick - Lea - Lea Green - Lea Gardens - Lea Church - Lea Road - Holloway - Florence Nightingale Memorial Hall - Mill Lane - John Smedley's - High Peak Junction Car Park.

 - 1:25,000 Outdoor Leisure Map No. 24 - The White Peak - East Sheet.

 and start - High Peak Junction Car park, beside the Cromford - Lea Bridge road. GR. SK313561.

 - Jug and Glass Inn, Lea; little over half way.

 Refreshments - High Peak Junction. The Coach House, Lea.

ABOUT THE WALK - The aim is to explore Holloway and Lea to see many of the places associated with Florence Nightingale and her family, together with a short side trip to see the exceptional church and hamlet of Dethick. First you walk along the Cromford Canal before following the Nightingale Arm to the canal wharf near Smedley's mill. From here you ascend Mill Lane - you descend it at the end - for a short distance before crossing fields around the western side of Lea Hurst. You ascend through Holloway to Upper Holloway and cross fields, with 360° views, to the eastern side of Lea to see Lea Hall. After a visit to Lea Chapel you cross a couple of fields to Dethick. You retrace your steps briefly before reaching

Lea near the Nightingale Cottages and Jug and Glass Inn. Following a path you walk around the northern edge of Lea Green to Long Lane with Lea Rhoderdendron Gardens to your right. You descend through woodland to Christ Church, Holloway and nearby Lea School. Following the road you enter Holloway to see a 19th century chapel, the Florence Nightingale Memorial Hall, historical plaque and Lea Holme. Here you regain Mill Lane and descend to Lea Bridge and John Smedley's Mill. A brief road and path walk returns you to the car park.

WALK INSTRUCTIONS - Exit the car park in the far top lefthand corner onto a path. In a few strides turn right over a footbridge over the River Derwent -the path to your left is your return one. Follow the path round and across the railway bridge and onto the Cromford Canal opposite the sheds and warehouse of the High Peak Railway Junction - museum and refreshments. Don't cross the canal but turn left to walk beside it on your right, passing the rail sheds on your right. Soon after the Leawood Pump House, on your left, and cross the aqueduct over the River Derwent. Just after turn left onto the Nightingale Arm, sign posted Lea Bridge 1/2 mile. The towpath keeps to the lefthand side of the canal, and crosses a former aqueduct over the railway (Matlock-Derby) line close to a tunnel. In little more than 1/4 mile reach Wharf Cottages and end of the arm. Continue ahead on the track and very soon pass on your right the western lodge of Lea Hurst with tall gates on the right. Keep ahead and reach the Lea Bridge road with Smedley's mill ahead.

Turn right and ascend Mill Lane - you will descend this at the end. In 200 yards pass the solitary house - Lamorbey - on the right. Just after on your left Hollins Wood Close. Opposite go through a kissing gate, by a path sign, and bear left and ascend the defined path by a wall on your left to a stile. Continue ahead on the now fenced path with deer on your right. Reach another stile and now level path with the perimeter wall and fence of Lea Hurst ahead. Bear left around the perimeter soon swinging right to cross the drive toLea Hurst. Cross via stiles and continue near the fence on your right to another stile with glimpses of Lea Hurst to your right. The path now turns left to Bracken Lane. Turn left and ascend towards Holloway but in 200 yards turn right, as footpath signed, and walk past Hebden House and other houses to your

26

left, to reach steps and ascend to Holloway-Crich road. Cross to your right to another path sign and follow the path into woodland and ascend numerous steps to Upper Holloway. Turn right and in a few yards gain a T. junction with the house, Muldavit, on the right. Turn left along Long Lane, with Upper Holloway Farm on your right.

Immediately past the farm, turn right over a stile by a path sign, and keep to the righthand side of the field as you ascend gently to a stile and path sign. From here you have extensive views over the Derwent Valley area and north-westerly to Riber Castle. Now following a track bear slightly left then right to the next stile. Keep ahead and cross the left side of a field to a stile and soon gain a track. Basically keep straight ahead for the next 1/4 mile as you walk along a walled path/track, which later becomes a sunken path to a stile. Keep ahead through a farm to Lea Moor Road. Your route is now left into Lea, but first turn right for a few yards to see the impressive north front of Lea Hall. Retrace your steps and continue into Lea. Soon pass a path sign - Tansley - on your right to Dethick - your next destination - but first, just ahead is Lea Chapel. Return to the stile and descend and cross the footbridge and ascend to a stile. Bear left and follow the defined path across two fields to Dethick church.

After you visit retrace your steps to the first stile and keep right on another path to a stile and woodland. Descend to another bridge and ascend steps to the road in Lea. Turn right and soon pass on your right the Nightingale Cottages and the Jug and Glass Inn. Here you turn left up Holt Lane, with children's pay area on the left. But first a little further along the road you pass The Coach House on your right and further on your left is Lea Green. Retrace your steps to Holt Lane and ascend, where it turns left, turn right to pass more houses and Holt House, here gain a walled path - footpath to Holloway - and walk around the perimeter wall of Lea Green on your right to Long Lane. To your right is Lea Gardens. Cross to your left and continue on a descending path through beech trees to pass above Christ Church, Holloway, and descend to the road. First turn right to visit the church and further along Lea School.

Retrace your steps and follow the road into Holloway, passing Smedley's Methodist Chapel - 1852 - on your right. Nearing the end of the road pass the Bakehouse and Coach House on your left before the junction with Mill Lane. Opposite is the Florence Nightingale Memorial Hall. Turn right down Mill Lane and in a few yards to your right is a Historical Notice board to many of the places you have seen on the walk. Continue down the lane and immediately pass Lea Holme on your right. Further down pass your earlier path and Hollins Wood Close. At the bottom turn right to see John Smedley's Mill and turn left back to the Cromford Road. Follow it for 1/4 mile to houses on your left and a righthand bend. Here leave the road onto a hedged path leading you back to the car park and start of the walk.

HISTORY NOTES IN WALKING ORDER -

HIGH PEAK JUNCTION - Because of the hilly terrain of the Peak District and considerable construction cost, a canal could not be made towards Manchester. Instead the canal's cargo was unloaded onto railway wagons and taken via nine inclines to the Peak Forest Canal at Whaley Bridge, 33 miles away; a journey of three days. The route was opened in 1831 and the last section ceased use in the 1960's. Today much of the line has been converted to a popular leisure trail.

CROMFORD CANAL - Completed in 1794 and engineered by William Jessop and Benjamin Outram, at a cost of £78,000. The 14 1/2 mile canal ran from Arkwright's mill at Cromford to Langley Mill to join the Erewash and Nottingham Canals. Today only the Erewash Canal is navigable. The 3,063 foot long Butterley Tunnel collapsed in 1900 basically cutting the canal in half, leading to its demise. The last section of the canal was in use until 1944. Today you can still walk the basic line of the canal and see many canal features along the way.

LEAWOOD PUMP HOUSE - Inside is a large beam engine built by Graham & Co of Elsecar, Yorkshire, and was installed in 1849. The canal was suffering from a lack of water and to alleviate the position water was pumped from the River Derwent into the canal. When operating the engine could lift 31 tons of water a minute. The pump house is open to the public on specific days, as detailed on the gate.

NIGHTINGALE ARM - Sometimes known as the Lea Wood Arm, as it runs beside Lea Wood. It was built by Peter Nightingale, Great Uncle of Florence, in 1800. Originally it stretched for 1/2 mile to Smedley's car park area at Lea Bridge, but in 1819 was shortened to Wharf Cottage. Here can be seen the wharf and base of the crane - an iron rim and central wooden boss in the stone. To the right of the cottage was where a hat factory existed, built in 1794. Military hats - "pill boxes" for the soldiers of the Crimean War were made here. The factory closed about 1860. Later the buildings were used as a wool warehouse and later by a Mineral water bottler, which ceased about 1906. - *"Mineral Waters and Soda Water Fountain from the celebrated Lea Wood Springs by John Else."* Beyond Smedley's Mill is the site of Cowhay Lead Works - owned by the Alsops and Wass families, operated until 1935. Lead ingots (pigs) and wool were transported by canal boat and incoming freight included coal and in 1854 4,000 tons were brought in. Originally, Smedley's Mill was a cotton mill built by Peter Nightingale in 1784. Later this was bought by John Smedley.

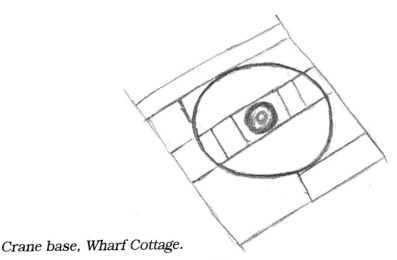

Crane base, Wharf Cottage.

Lea Hurst

LEA HURST - In 1707 the estate was bought by Thomas Nightingale. The gabled house dates from the 17th century, built by the Spateman's in about 1648, but was considerably enlarged by Florence's father, William Edward, in 1825. The estate remained in the Nightingale family until the death of Louis S. Nightingale in 1940. In 1946 the 200 acre estate was to be sold to Col. E. S. Halford, with the aim of turning into a nursing home in memory of Florence Nightingale. The plan never materialised and in 1951 the house was presented to the Royal Surgical Aid Society - founded in 1862 - for a home for the elderly by William Bowmer of the Wheatsheaf, Whatstandwell, who had bought it for £7,000. Today there are 26 residents with their own room and a resident Matron. The house still has considerable memorabilia of Florence, including drawings of her and her sister, Parthenope. There are also many of her letters, pictures and furniture. The house has an annual open day in July/August.

LEA HALL - The south front dates from the 17th century and includes parts of the early houses built about 1320 by John Rolleston. In the 17th century it was owned by the Peshalls who in 1648 sold it to John Spateman. His descendants sold it in 1707 to Thomas Nightingale - see Lea Hurst notes above. In 1754 Peter Nightingale added the beautiful five bay two story north front, with fluted Doric pilasters - one of the finest in Derbyshire. The architect is believed to be E. Stanley of Chesterfield. Florence's father lived here in 1825 while Lea Hurst was being enlarged and afterwards it was let. The Nightingale's sold the property in 1922.

LEA CHAPEL - Dates from 1690 and is today one of the oldest Non-Conformist chapels still in use today. It was endowed by Thomas Nightingale in 1732. The buildings was enlarged a century ago and the porch added in 1958.

DETHICK - Church dedicated to St. John the Baptist and basically remains unaltered since 1530. The hamlet is renowned for the Babington family, especially Thomas Babington for the plot to rescue Mary Queen of Scots. This led to his death. Many memorials to the Babington family can be seen in Ashover church.

NIGHTINGALE COTTAGES - As the date stone records, these were built by Peter Nightingale in 1781. Originally, as can be seen, there were six cottages; two of them have been made into one.

JUG AND GLASS INN - The date stone records S. S.E. 1782. Originally owned by the Nightingale family.

LEA GREEN - Began life as a large 15th century farmhouse. In 1839 it was rebuilt in neo-Jacobean style, set in 25 acres of gardens, for Joseph Wass, whose lead works was near Smedley's mill. In 1895 it was sold to J.B. Marsden-Smedley, the owner of Lea Mill, who considerably enlarged it in the early 1900's. Following his son's death in 1959 it was purchased by the Derbyshire Country Council for £10,500 and converted to a sports centre.

LEA GARDENS - The extensive Rhoderdendron gardens were began by J.B. Marsden-Smedley, and are open to public. In June they are a remarkable colourful sight.

LEA SCHOOL - The original school at Common End was built in 1808 by public subscription; the original foundation stone is incorporated in the present building. Florence's family financed the school except for a 2d charge per week per pupil. A larger school was needed and William Edward Nightingale (Florence's father) helped to raise and find a suitable spot for it; he gave £500 towards it. The school's location has often been described as, "One of the best village schools in the county." On completion on 7th September 1859, the school had 156 pupils. Edward Nightingale was a member of the Management Committee for many years, and helped with the appointment and salaries of the staff. The family also held an annual event at Lea Hurst, giving prizes and books to the pupils.

CHRIST CHURCH, HOLLOWAY - Built at the beginning of the 20th century and consecrated in 1903. The building cost £4,669 and built by J.W. Wildgoose of Matlock, on land given by the trustees of Mr. Shore Nightingale. Using an oak mallet made from an oak from Dethick Wood, Victor Cavendish M.P. laid the foundation stone. In 1904 the vicarage was added and six years later in 1910, the tower was built at a cost of £900, in memory of Mrs. Walker of Lea Wood Hall. (Lea Wood Hall is on the lefthand side of Mill Lane, as you descend.)

METHODIST CHAPEL, HOLLOWAY - Trinity chapel built in 1852 by John Smedley. In 1879 it was enlarged.

FLORENCE NIGHTINGALE MEMORIAL HALL - In 1927 Louis Shore Nightingale was made chairman of the committee to raise money for a hall. The land was a bequest of the Nightingale estate. On June 2nd. 1932 HRH Edward, Prince of Wales, laid the foundation stone. Nearly five months later on September 24th. 1932 it was opened; the building had cost £1,134 - 1s - 9d (£1134.9p). 150 chairs were purchased at a cost of 5s 6d (28p) each.

LEA HOLME - Popular with film makers for costume dramas. Once owned by Edward and Florence Nightingale. Later it was occupied by J.B. Marsden-Smedley before the enlargement of Lea Green had been completed.

The Florence Nightingale Museum

- situated on the site of St. Thomas' Hospital, is a treasure trove to the life and work of Florence Nightingale, and is very well worth a visit. The museum contains many of her artifacts, letters and clothes. There is a life-size reconstruction of a Crimean ward scene and a 20 mins audio-visual presentation. It is in easy walking distance from Westminster and Waterloo underground stations.

open - Monday to Friday - 10.00 - 17.00
Saturday, Sunday and Bank Holidays - 11.30 - 16.30

2, Lambeth Palace Road,
London. SE1 7EW

Tel. 020 7620 0374
Fax. 020 7928 1760

e-mail - curator@florence-nightingale.co.uk

Web site - www.florence-nightingale.co.uk

Reference Sources -

Dethick, Lea and Holloway - Childhood Reminisces - Vol. 1, 2 & 3 - Dethick, Lea and Holloway Historical Society. 1991.

Derbyshire Country House - Vol 1 and 2 - by Maxwell Craven and Michael Stanley. 1982.

The Derbyshire Home of Florence Nightingale. 1971.

The Life of Florence Nightingale by Sarah Tooley. Bowsfield. 1904.

Florence Nightingale by Phillippa Stewart. Wayland. 1973.

Florence Nightingale by D. Lammond. Duckworth 1935.

The Story of Florence Nightingale - The Heroine of the Crimea - by W.J.Wintle. The Sunday School Union.

Florence Nightingale and the Nurse Legacy by Monica Baley. 1986

The Private Life of Florence Nightingale by Richard Gordon. 1979.

Britain and the Crimea - 1855-56 - by J.B. Conacher. 1987.

The Banner of Battle: The Story of the Crimean War by Alan Palmer. 1987.

FAMOUS DERBYSHIRE PEOPLE SERIES
by John Merrill

- each guide book is 40 to 72 pages long, with the story of the person with maps, sketches and illustrations. Also in included is a detailed walk of about 4 to 5 miles around the area the subject lived, seeing at first hand where history was made.

SIR RICHARD ARKWRIGHT OF CROMFORD - the cotton spinning genius who revolutionised industry.

SIR JOSEPH PAXTON - Gardener to the Sixth Duke of Devonshire, who designed the village of Edensor and the Crystal Palace for the 1851 Great Exhibition.

FLORENCE NIGHTINGALE - The Lady with the lamp - the Heroine of the Crimea War and the founder of modern nursing.

JOHN SMEDLEY - The creator of Smedley's Hydro, Riber castle and Lea Mills.

BONNIE PRINCE CHARLIE - the story of march through Derbyshire to Derby, on his attempt to regain the English crown, in 1745. Includes walking instructions to the 21 mile "Bonnie Prince Charlie Walk", from Ashbourne to Derby.

THE STORY OF THE EARLS & DUKES OF DEVONSHIRE - The Cavendish family, from Bess of Hardwick through the Earls of Devonshire and the Dukes of Devonshire to the present time. Includes a walk around Chatsworth and Hardwick.

In preparation -

BESS OF HARDWICK - The Costly Countess - Builder of Hardwick Hall and "goaler" of Mary Queen of Scots.

MARY QUEEN OF SCOTS - "The Captive Queen" - The story of her fiften year imprisonment in Derbyshire, including the Babington Plot, before being beheaded.

John Merrill's - "My Derbyshire" Historical Series.

A TO Z GUIDE TO THE PEAK DISTRICT by John N. Merrill
WINSTER - A SOUVENIR GUIDE .by John N. Merrill
DERBYSHIRE INNS - an A TO Z GUIDE . by John N. Merrill
HALLS & CASTLES OF THE PEAK DISTRICT. by John N. Merrill.
DERBYSHIRE FACTS AND RECORDS by John N. Merrill
THE STORY OF THE EYAM PLAGUE by Clarence Daniel
THE EYAM DISCOVERY TRAIL by Clarence Daniel
PEAK DISTRICT SKETCHBOOKby John N. Merrill
LOST DERBYSHIRE VILLAGE WALKS - VOL 1 & 2 by John N. Merrill
TOURING THE PEAK DISTRICY & DERBYSHIRE BY CAR by John N. Merrill
LOST INDUSTRIES OF DERBYSHIRE by John N. Merrill
DERBYSHIRE LOST VILLAGE WALK - Vols. 1 & 2 by John N. Merrill
DESERTED MEDIEVAL VILLAGES OF DERBYSHIRE by John N. Merrill
MANORS & FAMILIES OF DERBYSHIRE - Vol 1 - A to L - Photographed & edited by
MANORS & FAMILES OF DERBYSHIRE -Vol 2 - M to Z - John N. Merrill
DERBYSHIRE PILGRIMAGES' by John N. Merrill

FAMOUS DERBYSHIRE PEOPLE - each includes a 4 mile historical walk.
SIR RICHARD ARKWRIGHT OF CROMFORD by John N. Merrill.
SIR JOSEPH PAXTON by John N. Merrill
FLORENCE NIGHTINGALE by John N. Merrill
JOHN SMEDLEY by John N. Merrill
MARY QUEEN OF SCOTS - "The Captive Queen." by John N. Merrill
BESS OF HARDWICK - "The Costly Countess" by John N. Merrill
THE STORY OF THE EARLS AND DUKES OF DEVONSHIRE by John N. Merrill
BONNIE PRINCE CHARLIE & 20 mile walk by John N. Merrill

GHOSTS & LEGENDS -
DERBYSHIRE FOLKLORE.by John N. Merrill.
DERBYSHIRE PUNISHMENT by John N. Merrill.
CUSTOMS OF THE PEAK DISTRICT & DERBYS by John N. Merrill
LEGENDS OF DERBYSHIRE. by John N. Merrill.
GRANDFATHER THOMAS JACKSON'S VICTORIAN CURES & RECIPES

PEAK DISTRICT VISITOR'S GUIDES by John N. Merrill
ASHOURNE   BAKEWELL   MATLOCK   THE HOPE VALLEY

DERBYSHIRE HISTORY THROUGH THE AGES -
Vol 1 - DERBYSHIRE IN PREHISTORIC TIMES & 13 mile walk by John N. Merrill
Vol 3 - DERBYSHIRE IN NORMAN TIMES by John N. Merrill
Vol 4 - DERBYSHIRE IN MONASTIC TIMES by John N. Merrill

OTHER JOHN MERRILL WALK BOOKS

CIRCULAR WALK GUIDES -
SHORT CIRCULAR WALKS IN THE PEAK DISTRICT - Vol. 1,2, 3 AND 9
CIRCULAR WALKS IN WESTERN PEAKLAND
SHORT CIRCULAR WALKS IN THE STAFFORDSHIRE MOORLANDS
SHORT CIRCULAR WALKS - TOWNS & VILLAGES OF THE PEAK DISTRICT
SHORT CIRCULAR WALKS AROUND MATLOCK
SHORT CIRCULAR WALKS IN "PEAK PRACTICE COUNTRY."
SHORT CIRCULAR WALKS IN THE DUKERIES
SHORT CIRCULAR WALKS IN SOUTH YORKSHIRE
SHORT CIRCULAR WALKS IN SOUTH DERBYSHIRE
SHORT CIRCULAR WALKS AROUND BUXTON
SHORT CIRCULAR WALKS AROUND WIRKSWORTH
SHORT CIRCULAR WALKS IN THE HOPE VALLEY
40 SHORT CIRCULAR WALKS IN THE PEAK DISTRICT
CIRCULAR WALKS ON KINDER & BLEAKLOW
SHORT CIRCULAR WALKS IN SOUTH NOTTINGHAMSHIRE
SHORT CIRCULAR WALKS IN CHESHIRE
SHORT CIRCULAR WALKS IN WEST YORKSHIRE
WHITE PEAK DISTRICT AIRCRAFT WRECKS
CIRCULAR WALKS IN THE DERBYSHIRE DALES
SHORT CIRCULAR WALKS FROM BAKEWELL
SHORT CIRCULAR WALKS IN LATHKILL DALE
CIRCULAR WALKS IN THE WHITE PEAK
SHORT CIRCULAR WALKS IN EAST DEVON
SHORT CIRCULAR WALKS AROUND HARROGATE
SHORT CIRCULAR WALKS IN CHARNWOOD FOREST
SHORT CIRCULAR WALKS AROUND CHESTERFIELD
SHORT CIRCULAR WALKS IN THE YORKS DALES - Vol 1 - SOUTHERN AREA.
SHORT CIRCULAR WALKS IN THE AMBER VALLEY (DERBYSHIRE)
SHORT CIRCULAR WALKS IN THE LAKE DISTRICT
SHORT CIRCULAR WALKS IN THE NORTH YORKSHIRE MOORS
SHORT CIRCULAR WALKS IN EAST STAFFORDSHIRE
LONG CIRCULAR WALKS IN THE PEAK DISTRICT - Vol.1, 2 , 3, 4 AND 5.
DARK PEAK AIRCRAFT WRECK WALKS
LONG CIRCULAR WALKS IN THE STAFFORDSHIRE MOORLANDS
LONG CIRCULAR WALKS IN CHESHIRE
WALKING THE TISSINGTON TRAIL
WALKING THE HIGH PEAK TRAIL
WALKING THE MONSAL TRAIL & SETT VALLEY TRAILS
PEAK DISTRICT WALKING - TEN "TEN MILER'S" - Vol One and Two
CLIMB THE PEAKS OF THE PEAK DISTRICT
PEAK DISTRICT WALK A MONTH Vols One,Two, Three, Four, Five & Six
TRAIN TO WALK Vol. One - The Hope Valley Line
DERBYSHIRE LOST VILLAGE WALKS -Vol One and Two.
CIRCULAR WALKS IN DOVEDALE AND THE MANIFOLD VALLEY
CIRCULAR WALKS AROUND GLOSSOP
WALKING THE LONGDENDALE TRAIL
WALKING THE UPPER DON TRAIL
SHORT CIRCULAR WALKS IN CANNOCK CHASE
CIRCULAR WALKS IN THE DERWENT VALLEY
WALKING THE TRAILS OF NORTH-EAST DERBYSHIRE
WALKING THE PENNINE BRIDLEWAY & CIRCULAR WALKS
SHORT CIRCULAR WALKS ON THE NEW RIVER & SOUTH-EAST HERTFORDSHIRE
SHORT CIRCULAR WALKS IN EPPING FOREST
WALKING THE STREETS OF LONDON
LONG CIRCULAR WALKS IN EASTERN HERTFORDSHIRE
LONG CIRCULAR WALKS IN WESTERN HERTFORDSHIRE
WALKS IN THE LONDON BOROUGH OF ENFIELD
WALKS IN THE LONDON BOROUGH OF BARNET
WALKS IN THE LONDON BOROUGH OF HARINGEY
WALK IN THE LONDON BOROUGH OF WALTHAM FOREST
SHORT CIRCULAR WALKS AROUND HERTFORD
THE BIG WALKS OF LONDON
SHORT CIRCULAR WALKS AROUND BISHOP'S STORTFORD
SHORT CIRCULAR WALKS AROUND EPPING

For a free complete catalogue of John Merrill walk Guides send a SAE to The John Merrill Foundation

CANAL WALKS -
VOL 1 - DERBYSHIRE & NOTTINGHAMSHIRE
VOL 2 - CHESHIRE & STAFFORDSHIRE
VOL 3 - STAFFORDSHIRE
VOL 4 - THE CHESHIRE RING
VOL 5 - THE GRANTHAM CANAL
VOL 6 - SOUTH YORKSHIRE
VOL 7 - THE TRENT & MERSEY CANAL
VOL 8 - WALKING THE DERBY CANAL RING
VOL 9 - WALKING THE LLANGOLLEN CANAL
VOL 10 - CIRCULAR WALKS ON THE CHESTERFIELD CANAL
VOL 11 - CIRCULAR WALKS ON THE CROMFORD CANAL
Vol.13 - SHORT CIRCULAR WALKS ON THE RIVER LEE NAVIGATION -Vol. 1 - NORTH
Vol. 14 - SHORT CIRCULAR WALKS ON THE RIVER STORT NAVIGATION
Vol.15 - SHORT CIRCULAR WALKS ON THE RIVER LEE NAVIGATION - Vol. 2 - SOUTH
Vol. 16 - WALKING THE CANALS OF LONDON
Vol 17 - WALKING THE RIVER LEE NAVIGATION
Vol. 20 - SHORT CIRCULAR WALKS IN THE COLNE VALLEY

Visit our website -
www.johnmerrillwalkguides.com

JOHN MERRILL DAY CHALLENGE WALKS -
WHITE PEAK CHALLENGE WALK
THE HAPPY HIKER - WHITE PEAK - CHALLENGE WALK No.2
DARK PEAK CHALLENGE WALK
PEAK DISTRICT END TO END WALKS
STAFFORDSHIRE MOORLANDS CHALLENGE WALK

THE LITTLE JOHN CHALLENGE WALK
YORKSHIRE DALES CHALLENGE WALK
NORTH YORKSHIRE MOORS CHALLENGE WALK
LAKELAND CHALLENGE WALK
THE RUTLAND WATER CHALLENGE WALK
MALVERN HILLS CHALLENGE WALK
THE SALTER'S WAY
THE SNOWDON CHALLENGE
CHARNWOOD FOREST CHALLENGE WALK
THREE COUNTIES CHALLENGE WALK (PEAK DISTRICT).
CAL-DER-WENT WALK by GEOFFREY CARR,
THE QUANTOCK WAY
BELVOIR WITCHES CHALLENGE WALK
THE CARNEDDAU CHALLENGE WALK
THE SWEET PEA CHALLENGE WALK
THE LINCOLNSHIRE WOLDS - BLACK DEATH - CHALLENGE WALK
JENNIFER'S CHALLENGE WALK
THE EPPING FOREST CHALLENGE WALK
THE THREE BOROUGH CHALLENGE WALK - NORTH LONDON

INSTRUCTION & RECORD -
HIKE TO BE FIT.....STROLLING WITH JOHN
THE JOHN MERRILL WALK RECORD BOOK
HIKE THE WORLD - JOHN MERRILL's guide to WALKING & BACKPACKING.

MULTIPLE DAY WALKS -
THE RIVERS'S WAY
PEAK DISTRICT: HIGH LEVEL ROUTE
PEAK DISTRICT MARATHONS
THE LIMEY WAY
THE PEAKLAND WAY
COMPO'S WAY by ALAN HILEY
THE BRIGHTON WAY by NORMAN WILLIS

THE PILGRIM WALKS SERIES -
THE WALSINGHAM WAY - ELY TO WALSINGHAM - 72 MILES
THE WALSINGHAM WAY - KINGS LYNN TO WALSINGHAM - 35 MILES
TURN LEFT AT GRANJA DE LA MORERUELA - 700 MILES
NORTH TO SANTIAGO DE COMPOSTELA, VIA FATIMA - 650 MILES
ST. OLAV'S WAY - OSLO TO TRONDHEIM - 400 MILES
ST. WINEFRIDE'S WAY - ST. ASAPH TO HOLYWELL
ST. ALBANS WAY - WALTHAM ABBEY TO ST. ALBANS - 26 MILES
ST. KENELM TRAIL by JOHN PRICE - CLENT HILLS TO WINCHCOMBE - 60 MILES
DERBYSHIRE PILGRIMAGES
LONDON TO CANTERBURY- 75 MILES
LONDON TO ST. ALBANS - 36 MILES
LONDON TO WALSINGHAM - 194 MILES
FOLKESTONE, HYTHE TO CANTERBURY - 25 MILES
THE JOHN SCHORNE PEREGRINATIONS - 27 MILES by M. MOONEY

COAST WALKS & NATIONAL TRAILS -
ISLE OF WIGHT COAST PATH
PEMBROKESHIRE COAST PATH
THE CLEVELAND WAY
WALKING ANGELSEY'S COASTLINE.
WALKING THE COASTLINE OF THE CHANNEL ISLANDS
THE ISLE OF MAN COASTAL PATH - "THE WAY OF THE GULL."
A WALK AROUND HAYLING ISLAND
A WALK AROUND THE ISLE OF SHEPPEY
A WALK AROUND THE ISLE OF JERSEY

DERBYSHIRE & PEAK DISTRICT HISTORICAL GUIDES -
A TO Z GUIDE OF THE PEAK DISTRICT
DERBYSHIRE INNS - AN A TO Z GUIDE
HALLS AND CASTLES OF THE PEAK DISTRICT & DERBYSHIRE
TOURING THE PEAK DISTRICT & DERBYSHIRE BY CAR
DERBYSHIRE FOLKLORE
PUNISHMENT IN DERBYSHIRE
CUSTOMS OF THE PEAK DISTRICT & DERBYSHIRE
WINSTER - A SOUVENIR GUIDE
ARKWRIGHT OF CROMFORD
LEGENDS OF DERBYSHIRE
DERBYSHIRE FACTS & RECORDS
TALES FROM THE MINES by GEOFFREY CARR
PEAK DISTRICT PLACE NAMES by MARTIN SPRAY
DERBYSHIRE THROUGH THE AGES - VOL 1 -DERBYSHIRE IN PREHISTORIC TIMES
SIR JOSEPH PAXTON
FLORENCE NIGHTINGALE
JOHN SMEDLEY
BONNIE PRINCE CHARLIE & 20 MILE WALK.
THE STORY OF THE EARLS AND DUKES OF DEVONSHIRE

JOHN MERRILL'S MAJOR WALKS -
TURN RIGHT AT LAND'S END
WITH MUSTARD ON MY BACK
TURN RIGHT AT DEATH VALLEY
EMERALD COAST WALK
I CHOSE TO WALK - WHY I WALK etc.
A WALK IN OHIO - 1,310 MILES AROUND THE BUCKEYE TRAIL.

SKETCH BOOKS -
SKETCHES OF THE PEAK DISTRICT

COLOUR BOOK:-
THE PEAK DISTRICT.......SOMETHING TO REMEMBER HER BY.

OVERSEAS GUIDES -
HIKING IN NEW MEXICO - VOL I - THE SANDIA AND MANZANO MOUNTAINS.
VOL 2 - HIKING "BILLY THE KID" COUNTRY. VOL 4 - N.W. AREA - "HIKING INDIAN COUNTRY."
"WALKING IN DRACULA COUNTRY" - ROMANIA.
WALKING THE TRAILS OF THE HONG KONG ISLANDS.

VISITOR GUIDES - MATLOCK . BAKEWELL. ASHBOURNE.